POSITION !
Pieces

for violin and piano
Easy repertoire in 2nd, 3rd and 4th positions

Neue Lagen für Violine und Klavier

Leichte Spielstücke in der zweiten, dritten und vierten Lage

All pieces edited and arranged by/herausgegeben und bearbeitet von

Marguerite Wilkinson and Alan Gout

FABER *ff* MUSIC

In order to achieve secure intonation, the student must understand the relative placings of the fingers across the strings when playing in different keys and positions. By 'staying put' in one position for a substantial stretch of music, the geography of that position is quickly learned, enabling the student to tackle the adventure of moving up and down the fingerboard with confidence.

These pieces have been chosen not only for this purpose, but also to present a wide variety of interesting and unusual repertoire from the baroque period to our own time. We hope that skill and enjoyment will thereby go hand in hand.

Marguerite Wilkinson
Alan Gout

Zur Erlangung einer sicheren Intonation braucht der Schüler Verständnis für die jeweilige Positionierung der Finger auf den Saiten bei unterschiedlichen Tonarten und Lagen. Dadurch, daß der Schüler sich in einem Musikstück über einen längeren Abschnitt hin in einer Lage bewegt, erlernt er den genauen Ort, die "Geographie" dieser Lage schnell. Mit diesen Kenntnissen ausgestattet kann er sich dann auch vertrauensvoll auf das Abenteuer einlassen, die Hand auf dem Griffbrett nach oben und unten zu bewegen.

Die vorliegenden Stücke wurden aber nicht nur aus diesem Grund, sondern auch ausgesucht, um eine große Breite interessanter und ungewöhnlicher Stücke vom Barock bis in unsere Zeit vorzustellen. Wir hoffen, daß das Erlernen technischer Fähigkeiten und der Spaß bei der Sache Hand in Hand gehen.

Marguerite Wilkinson
Alan Gout

All pieces © 1995 by Faber Music Ltd unless otherwise stated
This edition first published in 1995 by Faber Music Ltd
3 Queen Square London WC1N 3AU
Cover design by Lynette Williamson
Music processed by Wessex Music Services
German translations by Dorothee Göbel
Printed in England by Halstan and Co Ltd
All rights reserved

ISBN 0 571 51436 7

Carol

13th century

Allegro (♩ = 120)

German Folk Song

Johannes Brahms
(1833 - 1897)

3rd Position

Danish Folk Song

Traditional

Moderato (♩ = 92)

3rd Position

Piece

Edward Elgar
(1857 - 1934)

Allegro (♩ = 138)

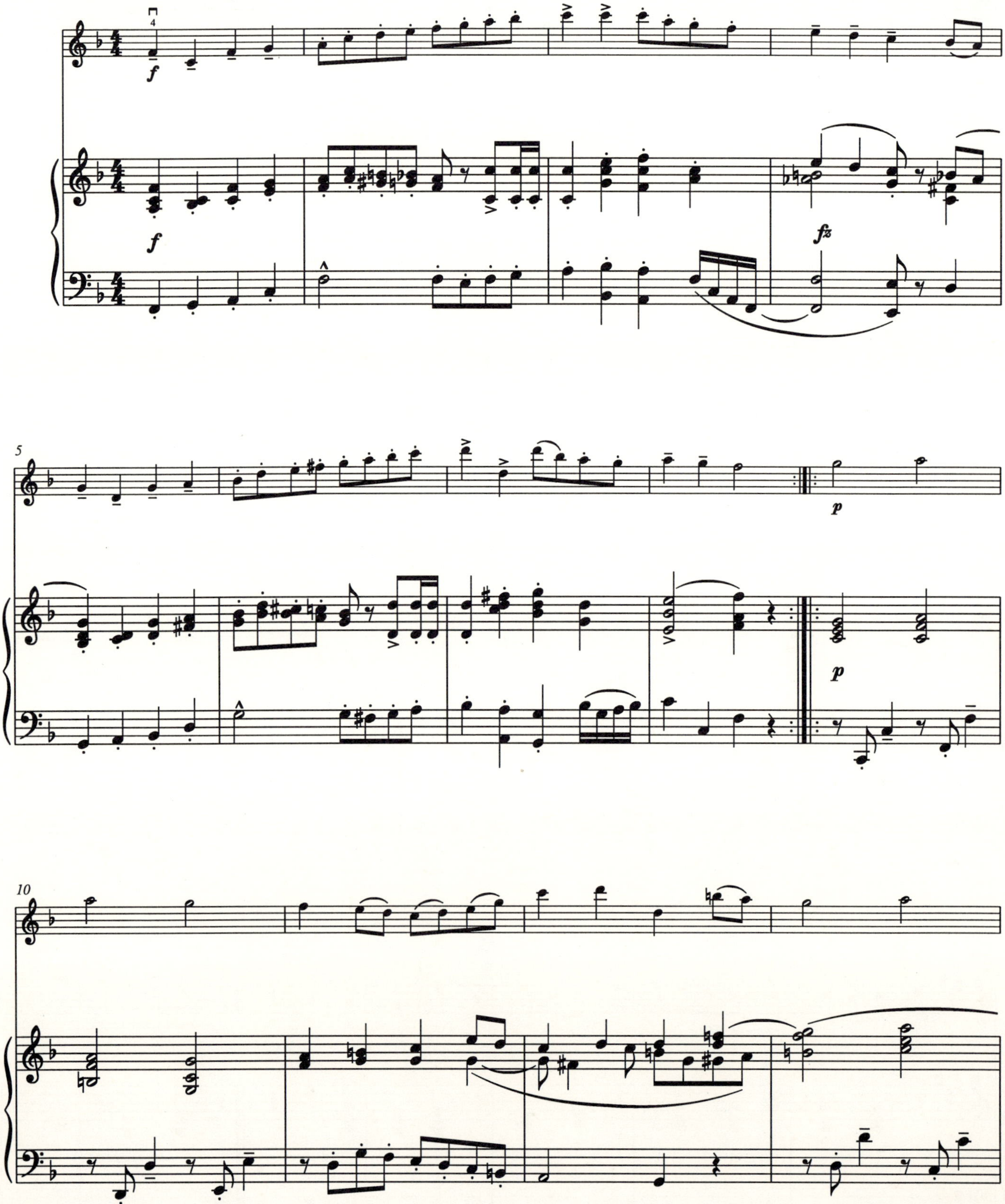

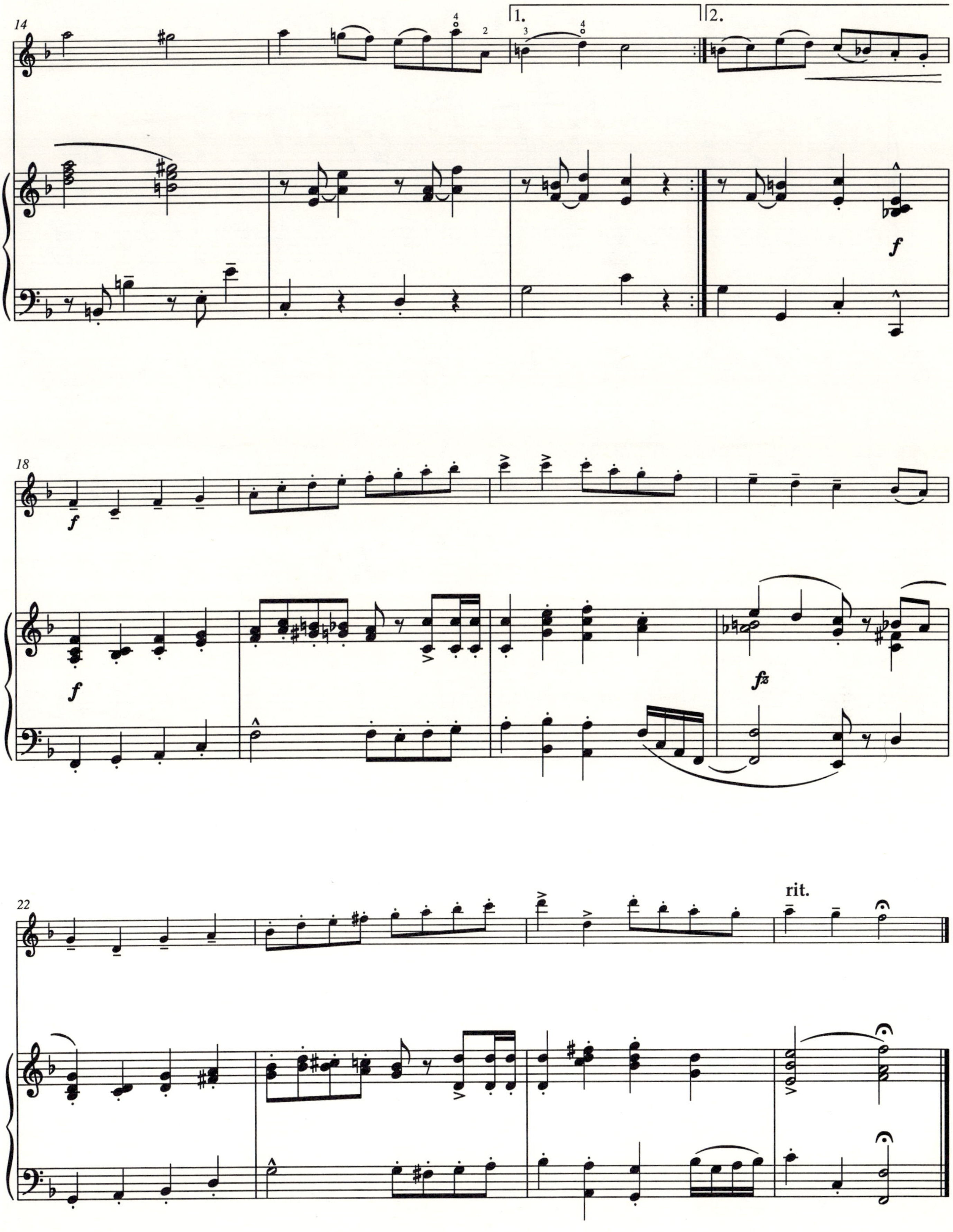
14
1.
2.
18
22
rit.

3rd Position

Largo (Balletto Op 1/5)

Domenico Gabrielli
(1651 - 1690)

* the top line of the accompaniment (mostly stems up) is the original 2nd violin part.

3rd Position

Rejoice, O Judah

G. F. Handel
(1685 - 1759)

8

3rd Position

Melody

Hans Georg Nägeli
(1773 - 1836)

Giocoso (♩. = 76)

2nd Position

The Flower of the County Down

Irish Air

Jaunty (♩ = 80)

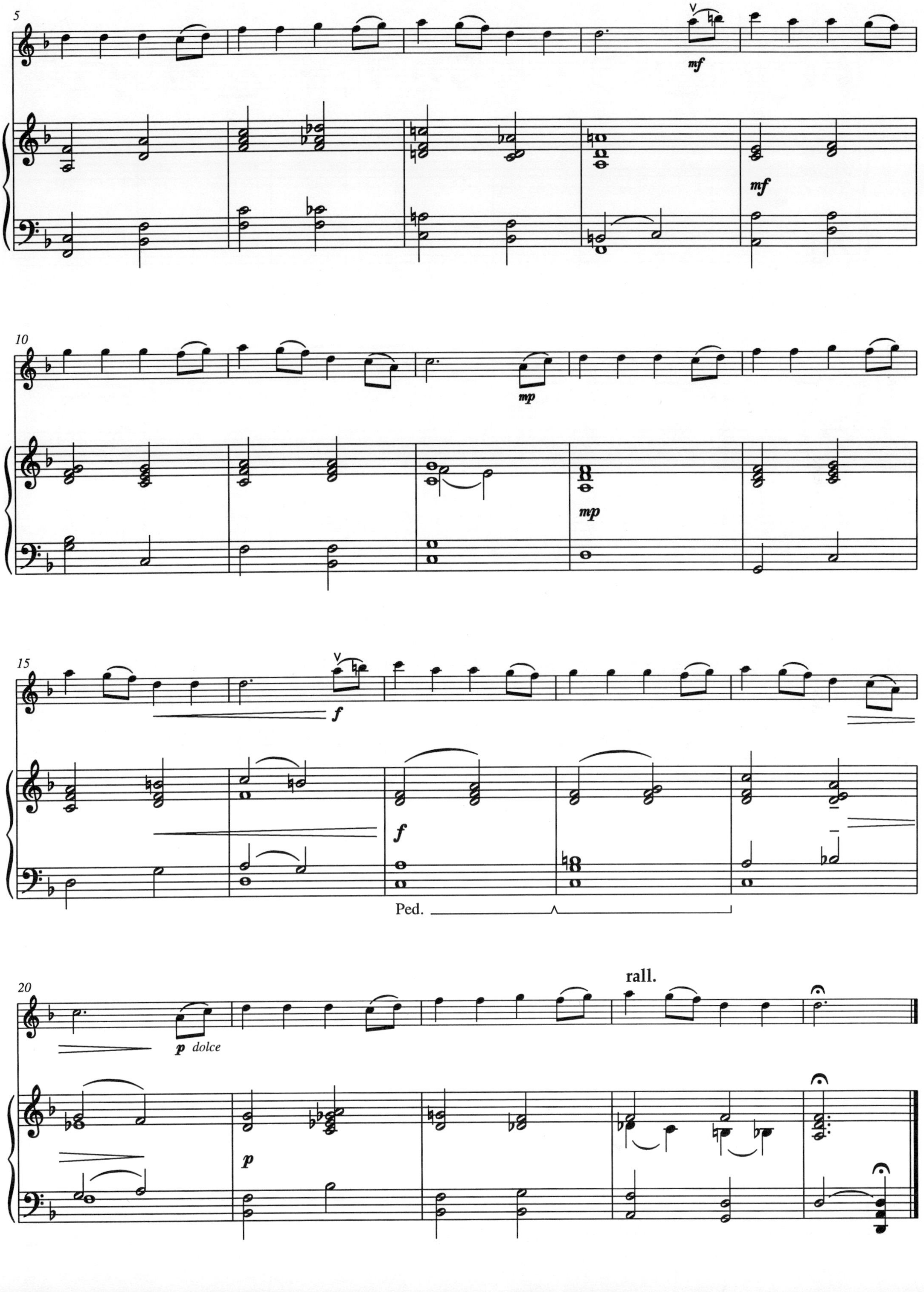
5
mf
mf
10
mp
mp
15
f
f
Ped.
20
p dolce
p
rall.

2nd Position

Oh dear, what can the matter be?

Vivace (♩. = 100)

Traditional

2nd Position

Iesu Cyfail F'Enaïd Cu
(Aberystwyth)

Joseph Parry
(1776 - 1851)

Slow (♩ = 72)

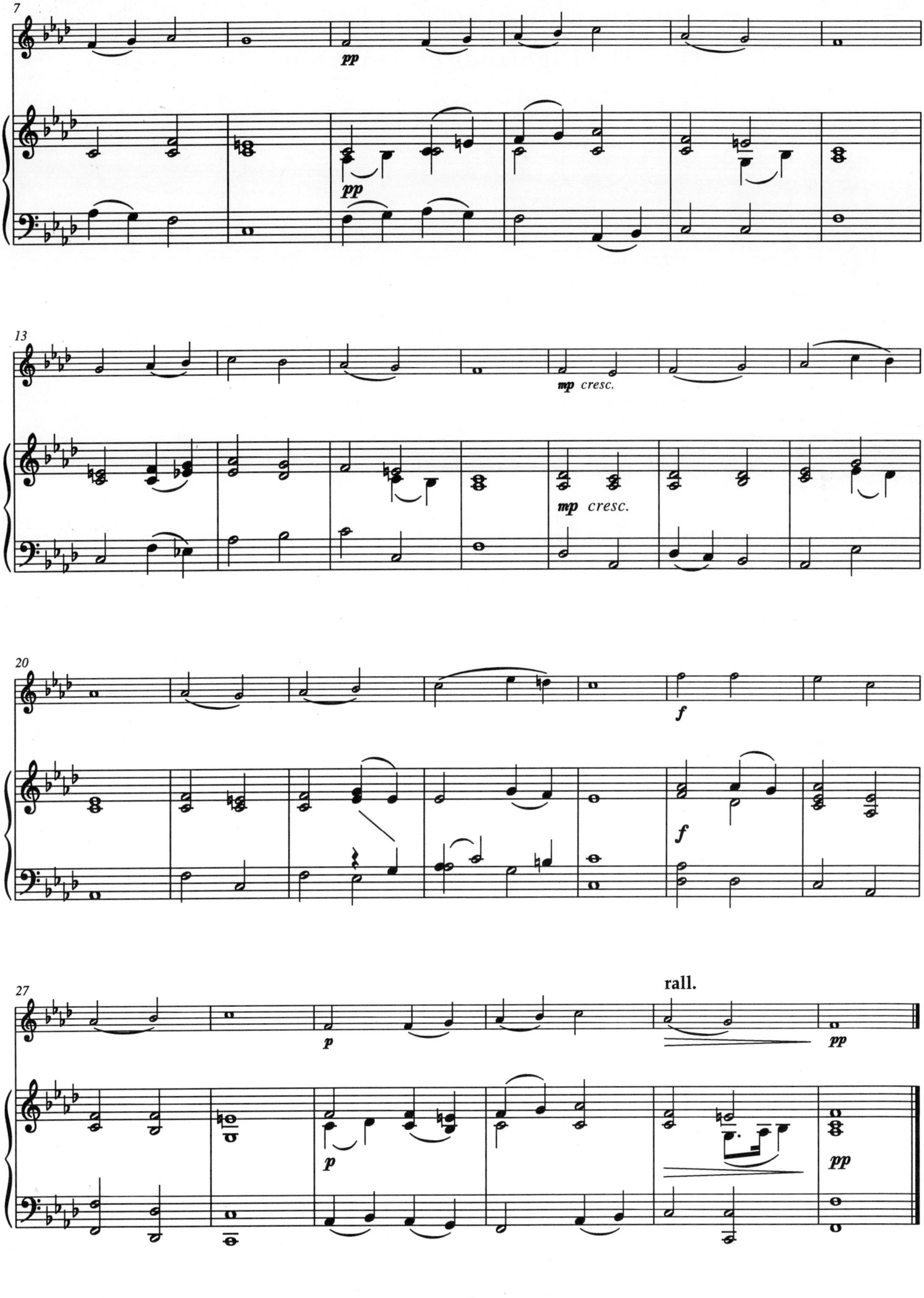
7
pp
pp
13
mp cresc.
mp cresc.
20
f
f
27
rall.
p
pp
p
pp

Strathspey
(The Highlands of Banffshire)

Moderato (♩ = 92)

Traditional

Arietta (from La Pescatrice)

2nd Position

Niccolò Piccinni
(1728 - 1800)

2nd Position

I got a Shoes

Spiritual

Con moto (♩ = 84)

2nd Position

Turkish Dance

Tempo giusto e marcato (♩ = 84)

Traditional

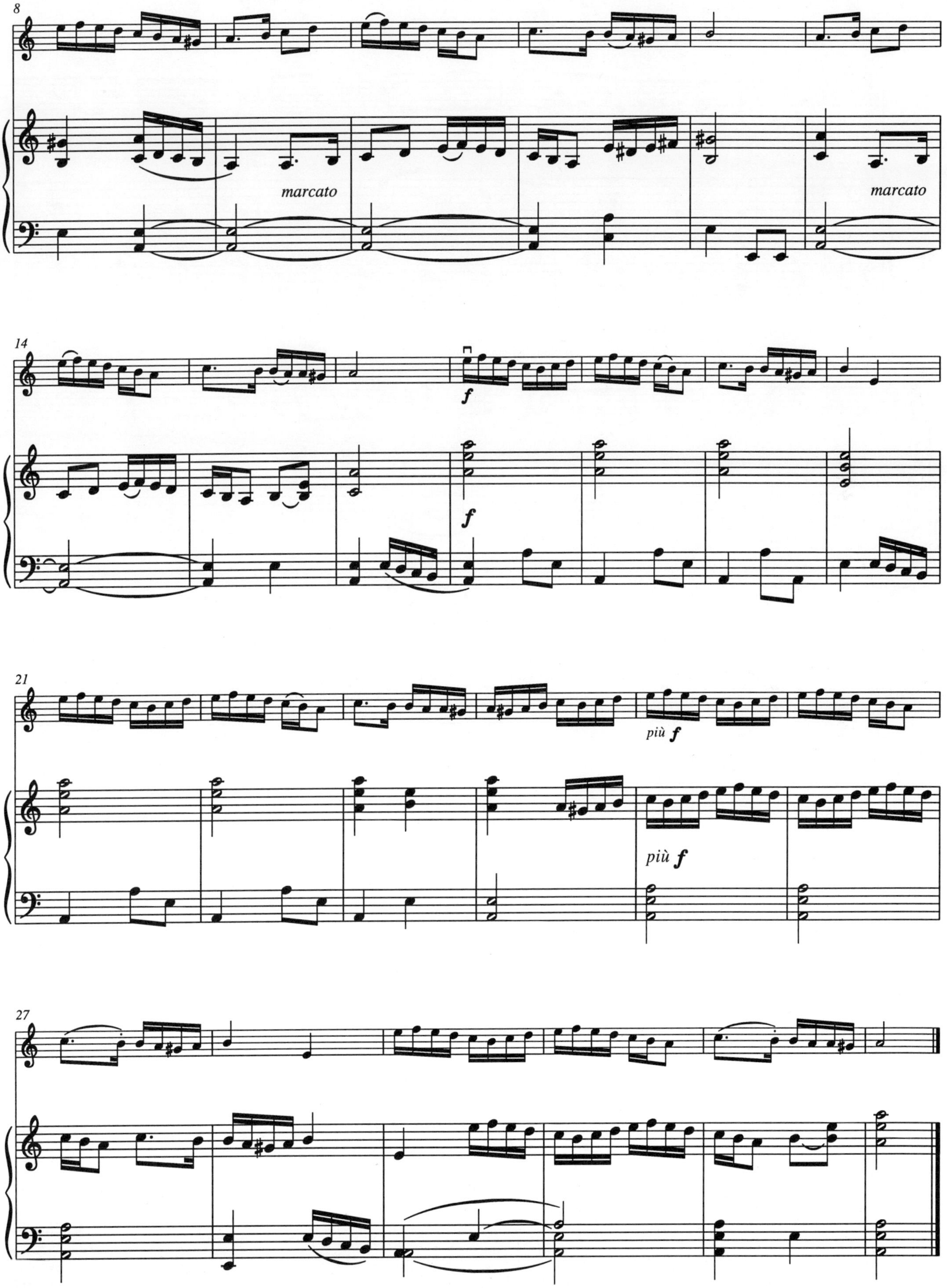
8
marcato
marcato
14
f
f
21
più f
più f
27

2nd Position

Mine Eyes have seen the Glory

W. Steffe
(fl. 19th century)

2nd, 3rd Positions

See, the Conquering Hero Comes

G. F. Handel
(1685 - 1759)

2nd & 3rd Position

Killarney

Moderato (♩ = 96)

M. W. Balfe
(1808 - 1870)

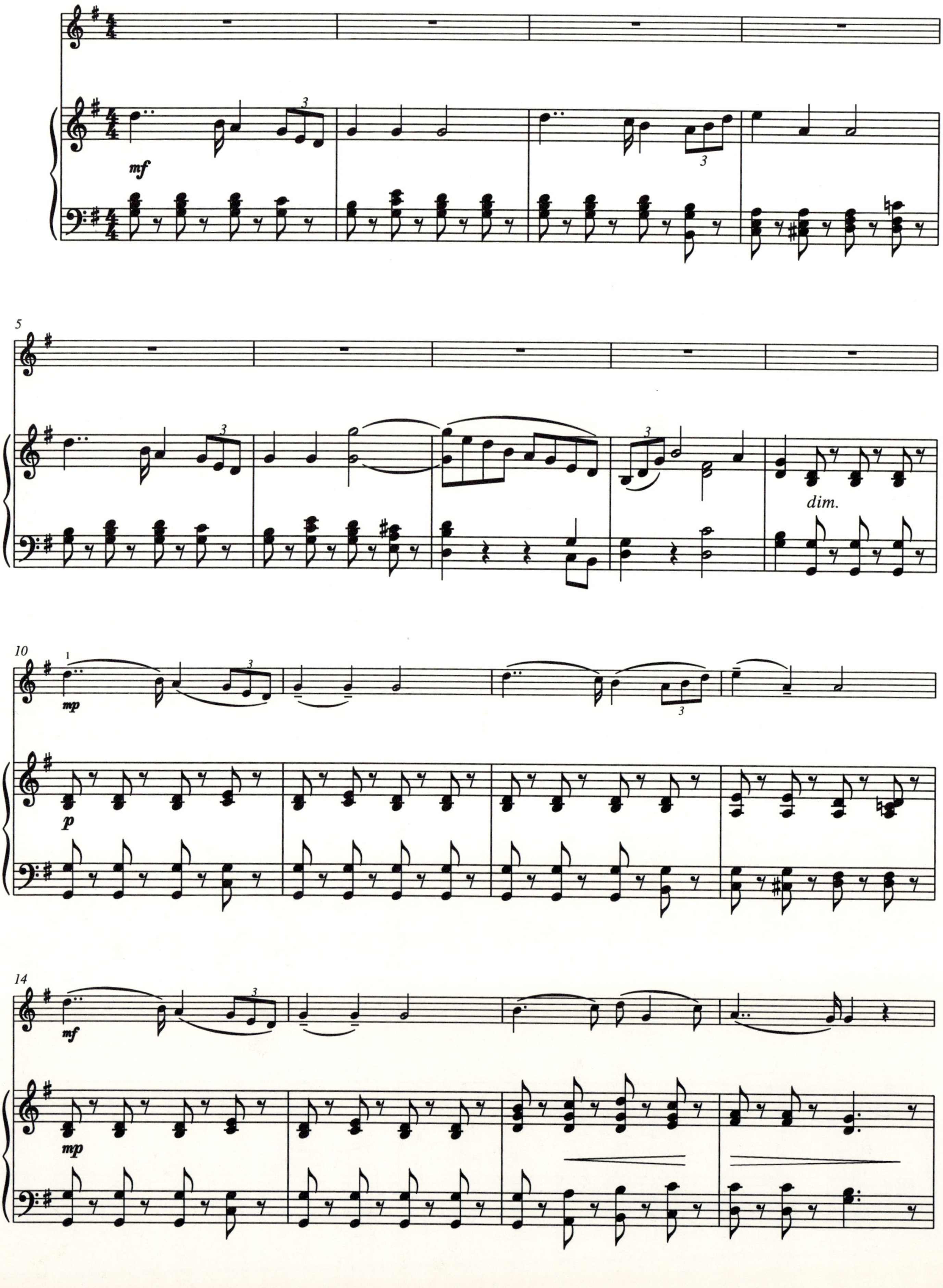

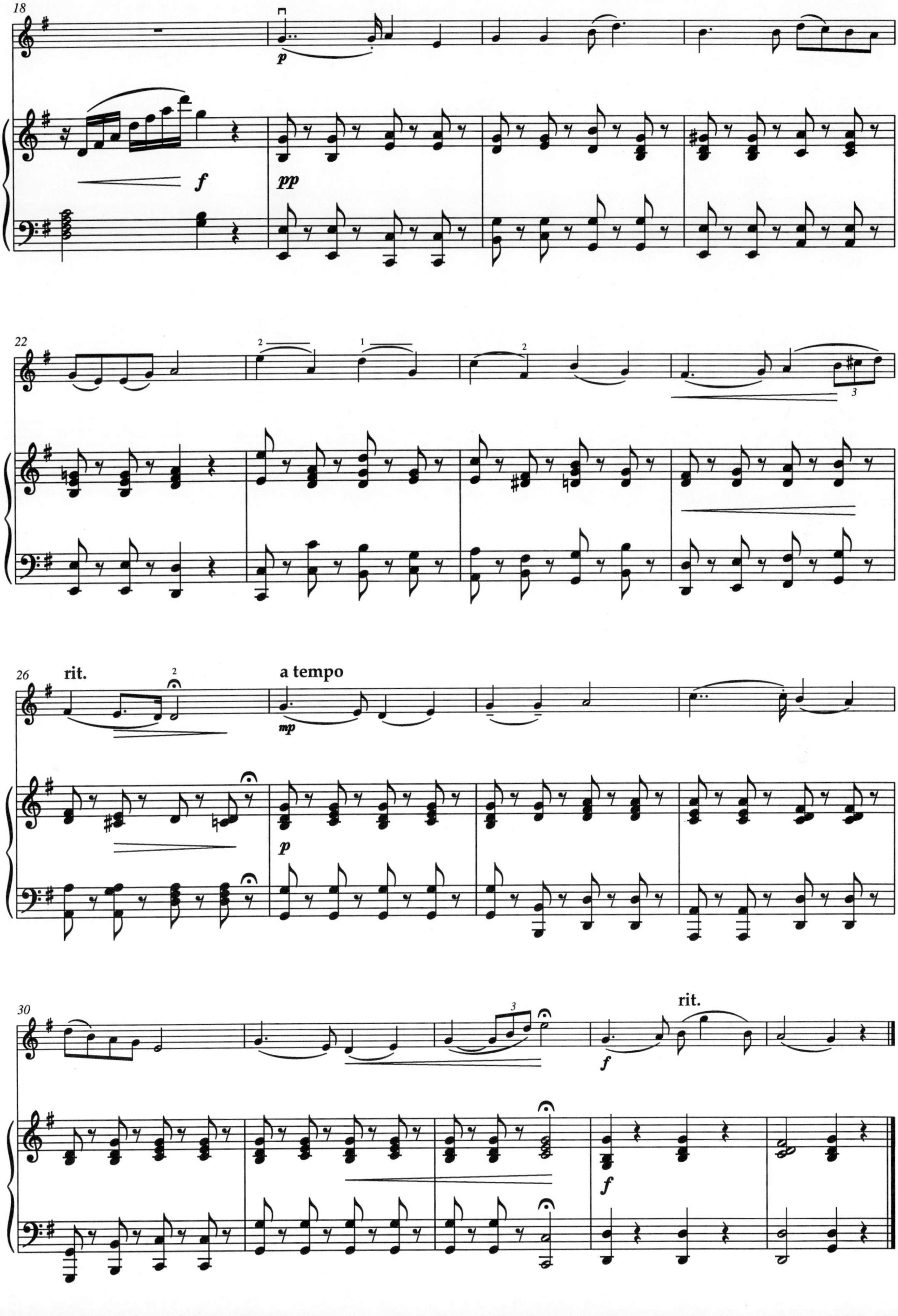
rit.
a tempo
rit.

2nd & 3rd Position

Pavane

Thoinot Arbeau
(1520 - 1595)
arr. Peter Warlock

Solenne (♩ = 54)

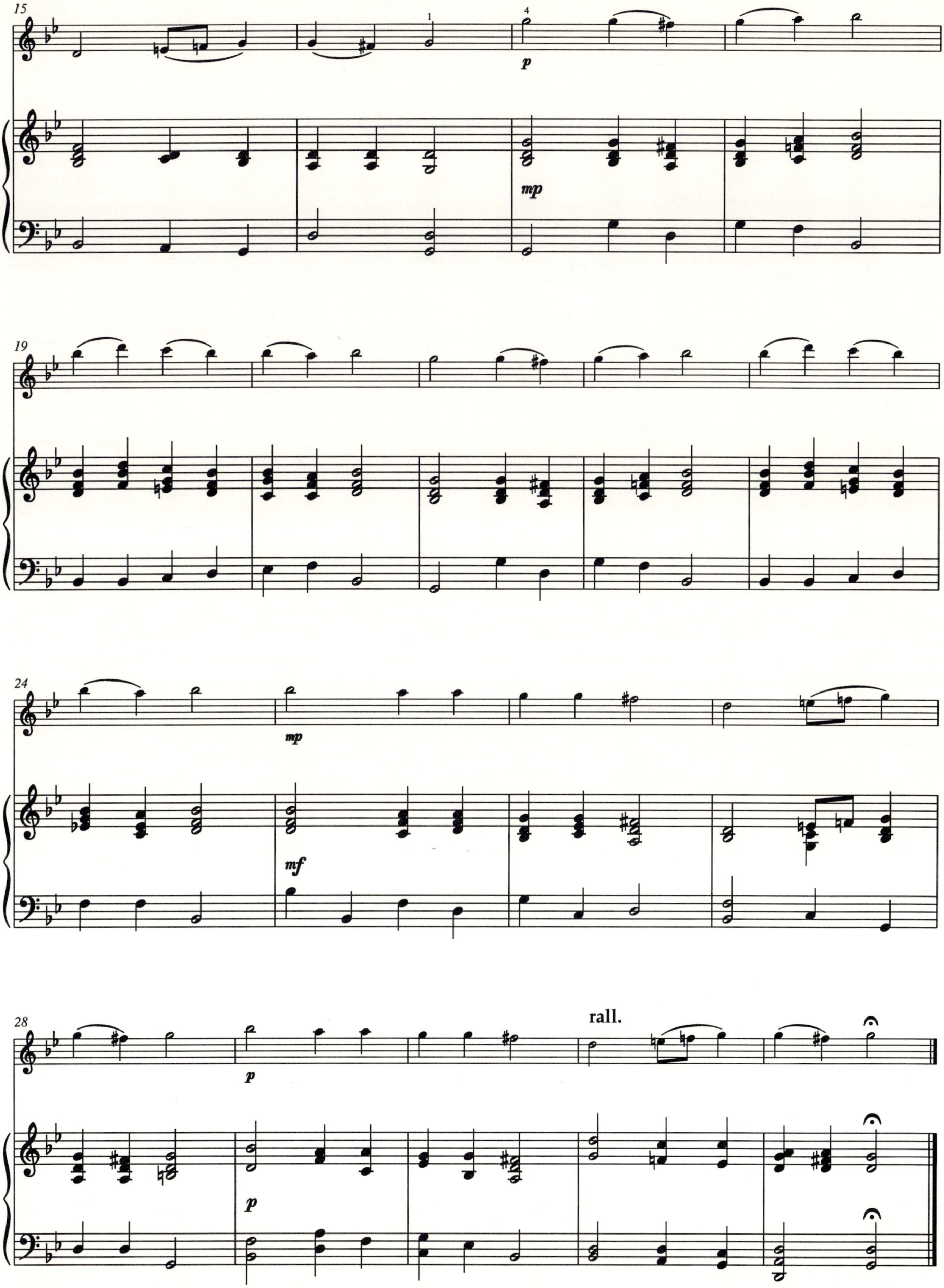
15
1
4
p
mp
19
24
mp
mf
28
p
p
rall.

3rd & 4th Position

Sua Alemanda

Domenico Gabrielli
(1651 - 1690)

* the top line of the accompaniment (stems up) is the original 2nd violin part.